MODERN PUBLISHING'S UNAUTHORIZED BIOGRAPHY OF

JASON PRIESTLEY

by
Donna Unangst

D1310199

Modern Publishing
A Division of Unisystems, Inc.
New York, New York 10022

Printed in the U.S.A.

PHOTO CREDITS: Pages 47 and 59 Vinnie Zuffante/Star File Photo; page 59 Star File Photo; pages 5, 21 and 53 Smeal/Galella, Ltd.; page 8 AP/Wide World Photos; Front Cover and page 9 Lori Stoll/Retna; pages 23 and 33 Steve Granitz/Retna; pages 10 and 24 Movie Star News; page 45 Robert Karpa/Outline Press; page 35 Angie Coqueran/LFI; page 16 Michael Ferguson/Globe Photos, Inc.; page 18 Robin Platzer/Twin Images; page 38 Bill Rediger/Shooting Star; pages 30 and 42 Mark Sennet/Onyx; Back cover, title page and pages 12, 14, 17, 27, 29, 40, 48 © Fox Broadcasting Company

Cover and Interior Book Design by: Bob Feldgus

Book Number: 10620
ISBN Number: 1-56144-127-9

CONTENTS

INTRODUCTION

Jason Priestley, who stars as Brandon Walsh on Fox TV's hottest show, "Beverly Hills, 90210," is the newest heartthrob on the scene! Ever since "90210" hit the airwaves last fall, teens everywhere have been going crazy over Jason and his sensitive portrayal of teen Brandon Walsh. With each new episode of "Beverly Hills, 90210," the show gains zillions more viewers and Jason's fan mail (which numbers an amazing hundred letters a day) grows even greater!

Just what is it about "90210" that makes so many people tune in every week? Chances are it's lots of things, but as the star of the show, Jason is the main draw! What is it about Jason that makes him so special? He's gorgeous, one of *People* magazine's "50 Most Beautiful People In The World" last year in fact, but seeing Jason act for even five minutes proves that there is more to this talented twenty-three-year-old than meets the eye.

As Jason gets more popular with every week that goes by, more of you want to know just what television's newest star is all about. Are you curious about what Jason was like growing up? Interested in what he likes to do when he's not "being" Brandon Walsh? Want to know what it's like working on television's hottest show? How about Jason's plans for the future and what he feels about his sudden success? Then you've come to the right place.

On these pages we'll be taking a close-up look at the real Jason Priestley. You'll learn everything there is to know about Brandon Walsh's alter-ego. You'll be getting an insider's peek at what Jason is all about, the Jason that only close friends usually get to see. So fasten your seatbelts and get ready to go!

One last thing—read carefully, because you will be

tested. Okay, so it won't be like a history exam, but there is a super-tricky trivia quiz on Jason and "90210" at the end of the book. Good luck with it!

What are you waiting for?

Dressed to the nines, Jason is as handsome as ever.

JASON!

Jason Priestley was born on August 28, 1968 in a city in Canada called Vancouver. He is the youngest of two children. Jason's sister, who is eighteen months older than he, is a student in London, England. Jason's parents are divorced; his mother, a former ballet dancer and choreographer, is now a real estate agent in Vancouver; his father is a representative for a furniture and textile company in Vancouver. Jason also has two stepsisters back home in Canada. His parents separated when he was young; Jason lived with his mother until he was sixteen and credits her with giving him "a great sense of independence." Jason then lived with his father during the last two years of high school.

The Priestley-clan has historically been an athletic one. His older sister is a dancer, like his mom. His grandfather was even an acrobat in the circus! For Jason this athletic talent showed itself in the form of hockey. From the time Jason was old enough to walk he could ice skate; from there it was just a hop, skip and jump into playing hockey with his friends, who call him by the nickname "J." J would get up at the crack of dawn, sling his blades over his shoulder and head out the door to meet his friends at a nearby pond or rink. Not only did Jason play hockey, he excelled at it, consistently being named MVP of every team he played on and leading those teams to victory.

When he wasn't out on the ice, Jason found lots of other sports to keep him busy. Jason snow skiied, and played a rough-and-tumble sport called rugby. Being athletic had its downfalls too, Jason explains, "As a kid, not a day went by that I didn't come home with a cut, bump, bruise, or broken bone. I gave my mother many early heart attacks!"

As if Jason wasn't expending enough energy playing every sport under the sun, one day while watching television, he spotted some kids on a television commercial.

From that point on, the 4-year-old-Jason begged his mother every day to let him try acting!

Finally, his mom relented and took J to her former agent. Within weeks, Jason was working in local commercials. By the age of eight, Jason had landed his first major role, in a made-for-television movie called "Stacey," for the Canadian Broadcasting Corporation.

Jason continued to get regular acting jobs while growing up, and even took some classical acting training workshops under famous instructors Howard Fine and June Whitaker, at the Neighborhood Playhouse. He also continued with his hockey playing as well. Then, for a period in high school, Jason gave up acting. He decided he wanted to be a regular teenager. "I didn't want to have to worry about losing a job if I cut my hair or got a cut on my face," Jason explains. One of the first things Jason did after quitting acting was get a modified mohawk hairstyle, just because now he could! What a crazy guy!

At high school graduation, Jason decided that acting really was what he wanted to do with his life. (His hair had grown back!) So, with all the money he had saved from acting jobs in Canada, Jason moved to Los Angeles. He got a small apartment there and soon began working regularly onstage, in television and doing small parts in feature films.

During those first few months in Los Angeles, Jason appeared on the television shows "MacGyver, "Quantum Leap," "21 Jump Street" and "Airwolf." He appeared in the plays "The Breakfast Club," "Rebel Without A Cause" and "Addict." Jason also landed parts in the big-screen flicks "Watchers," "The Boy Who Could Fly" and "Nowhere To Run." Then came a series of big breaks that led to his playing Brandon Walsh.

Jason nabbed the prime role of the school hunk in a movie for Disney called "Teen Angel." He was also cast in the sequel, "Teen Angel Returns." Both of these movies were serials; that means they were broken into lots of little parts and shown on episodes of "The New

Then and now ... wow! At left, Jason as he appeared in the TV show "Sister Kate" and, at right, as Brandon Walsh on "Beverly Hills, 90210."

Mickey Mouse Club." Based on his performances in these widely-seen pieces, Jason landed the role of or-

phan Todd Mahaffey in the network television show, "Sister Kate." "Sister Kate" is in syndication now. On the show, Stephanie Beacham, who now plays Dylan McKay's mom on "90210," plays a nun who gets stuck taking care of a group of orphans. The show didn't last

Jason's primetime TV exposure began on the show "Sister Kate."

long, but it lasted long enough for one very key person to see it.

Producer Aaron Spelling is responsible for such

smash television hits as "The Love Boat" and "Charlie's Angels," shows that Jason says he "grew up on." Spelling has a teenage daughter named Tori, who now plays Donna Martin on "90210." When Tori's dad was casting his newest show, about high school students from Minneapolis transplanted to Beverly Hills, he was having difficulty finding a young actor to play the starring role, a male in a fraternal set of twins. Fate stepped in. Tori was a huge fan of "Sister Kate," and of Jason in particular, and recommended him for the role of Brandon. Jason tested for and got the part.

"Beverly Hills, 90210" started its run last fall in stiff competition with a ton of other school-oriented shows. Remember "Hull High"? "Ferris Bueller"? They were dropped soon after the season began, but "90210" made the grade. At first, the show was near the bottom of the ratings, but Jason and the other cast members of "90210" took charge with stories that soon had every teen in America turning in. Before long, Jason was appearing on every magazine cover and talk show, letting the rest of the world in on a secret American teens had known since the very first episode of "Beverly Hills, 90210"—not only is Jason gorgeous, he's incredibly talented too!

A DAY IN THE LIFE OF JASON!

One thing's for sure, Jason Priestley's busy as can be! Being on a top-rated television show every week may seem like a glamorous, easy life, but guess what? It's lots of hard work, too! Each one-hour episode of "Beverly Hills, 90210" that you see takes one whole week to make! Can you imagine?! And, since "90210" is one of the few shows that aired new episodes instead of reruns during the summer season, that means that the "90210" bunch works even harder than most other TV stars!

Curious about what a super-hardworking actor like Jason does during a day? Read on!

Rrrrrrrrring! It's 6:30 in the morning in J's three-bedroom house in Woodland Hills, California. Jason loves

No wonder the cast of "Beverly Hills, 90210" is all smiles—the program is teen viewers' top choice for TV drama!

waking up to the radio, so his alarm clock's set to California's alternative rock station, KROQ. Each and every day, Jason opens his eyes to tunes by his fave performers, folks like England's Jesus Jones and EMF, as well as America's The Replacements and Jane's Addiction.

Next up for J? An ice-cold shower and shave, so that he is stubble-less and ready to be Brandon Walsh. Jason doesn't style his hair before a day on the set because it gets re-done as soon as he arrives. Jason's a very casual dresser so he'll zip into a pair of his fave jeans, a T-shirt and maybe a vest. Then he'll finish off with a pair of hightops or combat boots. Keep in mind that Jason's got to be extra quiet in the a.m. because he lives with his buddy, actor David Sherill, who you may remember from the Charlie Sheen flick, "The Rookie." Dave doesn't have to be up until quite a bit after J!

On into the kitchen where Jason's coffeemaker has already gotten a few cups of his fave morning beverage ready! Grabbing a cup of coffee (no breakfast at home for Jason, who jokes that the only thing in his bachelor's refrigerator is a bottle of ketchup!), Jason plops down at his kitchen table and quickly glances over his copy of that week's "90210" script. Since Jason is one of the show's stars, he works almost every day when the show is filming. After double-checking the day's lines, which he memorized the night before, Jason's up and ready to go!

First though, a peek in on his pet—a pig! It's a domesticated variety called a "pot belly," which co-star pal Luke Perry also owns. Jason gives his little friend some fresh water and food and turns out the lights. Jason and Dave used to have a dog, but one day the dog wandered out and never came back. That pooch didn't know what he'd be missing out on!

Jason heads out to his Nissan Pathfinder truck and starts up the motor. Backing his truck out into the street, Jason turns on the radio to groove to a few tunes and catch up on what's happening in the world. Next it's on to the extremely busy L.A. freeways for the twenty-or-so minute ride to the secret location where the show tapes. Jason is instructed the day before where the first scene of the day will be shot. For example, the show's outside shots (walking into school, etc.) are done at a high school in Torrance, but all the indoor shots are done in a warehouse! Special locations are sometimes used, for episodes like the ones where the gang visits David Silver's grandparents in Palm Springs or the summer episodes that took place at the beach. It's extremely

Back-to-back babes! Luke and Jason forever!

important Jason knows exactly where he's headed when he leaves the house—after all, the show can't go on without its star!

Jason usually arrives on the set between 7:00 and 7:15 for what is known as the 8:00 call. That means the show's producers want J on the set and in costume and makeup by 8:00! Depending on what's required for the day, Jason's hair and makeup, like that of most of the guys on the show, only takes about a half-hour or so.

Makeup? Jason? That's right. Even though J is obviously naturally gorgeous, the harsh lights of television demand all actors wear at least some makeup so their faces don't wash out on camera. Generally, Jason only requires a light flesh-colored base. Next, the show's hairstylist checks Jason's coif. His sideburns and hair will be trimmed if they need to be and his hair is washed and blown dry, à la Brandon. When he's not working, Jason sometimes likes to grow his hair and a slight beard so he can go out in public unrecognized! But, for the show, it is important that Brandon look the same from week to week. After makeup, Jason has a couple minutes to bop around the set, greeting the cast and crew before heading into the costume department.

On into costume! While Jason prefers a more adventurous look (leather jackets, funky tees) when he's not on set, Brandon is a pretty conservative character. His seriously clean-cut, preppy clothes are chosen by the show's fashion stylist, who shops for the entire cast's wardrobe. Hair and makeup done, Brandon Walsh-like duds in place, Jason heads out for this first scene!

Being on the set of "Beverly Hills, 90210" may seem more like a big party than a job, but it's both working and playing that are getting done! Since a lot of the show's cast is close in age, there's a special family-like atmosphere on the set that everyone in the cast mentions. Luke Perry, who plays Dylan McKay, says, "This is the first time I've worked with a cast where we're forced to relate this closely. We spend sixty hours a week together. I wouldn't trade these guys for anything!" Tori Spelling, who plays Donna Martin, agrees. "The cast is like my second family," she says. "I've always wanted an older brother and now I have two, Luke and Jason!"

Curious about some behind-the-scenes "90210" hijinx?

Carol Potter plays Jason's television mother, Cindy Walsh. She sums it up, "I'm definitely the one with the reputation of being more serious than anyone else! The boys are just irrepressible! Jason is the most wisecracking, he even has the edge over Jim Eckhouse, who plays my husband. But they keep a good competition going there!"

Jason attended the birthday bash for superstar Helen Hayes.

The joking around, of which Jason is the biggest culprit, makes the ultra long days of shooting go faster. It is typical for the "90210" bunch to shoot from 8:00 in the

Jason's TV family co-stars: Shannen Doherty, Carol Potter, and James Eckhouse.

morning until 10:00 or so at night! The only rest comes during one-hour breaks for lunch and dinner, when whoever is on the set that day heads into the show's cafeteria for some chow. Music blasts, usually courtesy of Brian Austin Green. He plays the on-show deejay and loves mixing tunes in real life as well!

First the actors in the scene read through the lines and ask the director questions. For example: if the writer of that week's episode has Jason saying something the actor thinks Brandon wouldn't say, Jason brings the point up for change. Then the actors work out something called blocking, when it's decided who should stand where for the best lighting and camera shots. Only then is the scene done for the camera to record. Normally, the scene is acted out and taped several times, so that the editor has a choice of "takes" to use for the finished episode. A typical scene may take up to four or five hours to get right!

After all the scenes for the day are done, the cast heads home. After all, the next day they usually have to get up at the crack of dawn to do it all over again! So, into his Nissan Jason goes for the drive home. Once

"Parker Lewis Can't Lose" star Billy Jayne and Jason pose for a pic.

there, it's not unusual for him to head straight for bed, where he'll read over and memorize the next day's scenes. Around midnight or so it's lights out for J!

KICKING BACK WITH JASON!

Now you know that Jason is one of the hardest-working actors around. The nearly year-round shooting schedule of "90210" keeps him hopping pretty much all the time. But when Jason does have some free time what does he do? Well, he's got a bunch of interests ranging from cooking to the sport of bungee jumping!

When Jason is shooting, he works anywhere from 10 to 14 hours a day, Monday to Friday, on each episode of "90210"! That leaves Jason Saturdays and Sundays for kicking back and doing the other things he likes to do. Jason manages to pack plenty of activity into those two days!

When the weather's nice outside, you're likely to find Jason cruising around the great outdoors on his Yamaha motorcycle. Driving around the hills and mountains in California with the wind blowing through his hair is one of Jason's favorite ways to unwind! Jason's pal/co-star Luke also has a motorcycle (his is a Harley-Davidson) and the two gorgeous stars sometimes pack provisions and take their bikes out for an overnight trip! Once Jason even brought his motorcycle to the set of "90210" and, as a prank, drove the Yamaha down the hallway of the "school"! Needless to say, that take never made it into the episode when it was aired!

Growing up in the beautiful country surrounding the Canadian city of Vancouver, Jason developed a love of sports. You know that he adores ice hockey and has been playing since he was old enough to wear skates ... but did you know that he also skis, golfs, plays tennis and basketball, and is a lover of a game called rugby, which is a sort of soccer-meets-football sport? J loves spending as much time as possible participating in athletics. Basically, he's just a really energetic guy!

Another of Jason's free-time passions is movies! He loves going out to the movies or just renting videos. Some of his favorite actors are action heroes like Rutger Hauer and James Woods and quirky guys like Gary Oldman and Dennis Hopper, as well as classic talents, like Al Pacino and Robert Duvall. Jason says he loves watching flicks these dudes are in because he "tries to reach their level" when he performs!

Jason combines his love for movies with the opportunity to get out and meet his fellow actors at movie premieres. Jason's always popping up at the latest and hottest flicks opening in Tinseltown! He's been spotted at every event from the opening of "City Slickers," where he hung out with Lou Diamond Phillips of "Young Guns II," to the re-release of Kirk Douglas' all-time classic, "Spartacus," after which Jason joked to the attending press, "What a great movie! I'm going to open a store that sells tunics, like the ones in the movie, on Melrose Avenue!"

And speaking of going out in the public eye, Jason never turns down the chance to represent "Beverly Hills, 90210" at a television awards show! At this year's Emmy Awards (which are presented for outstanding achievement in television), Jason, looking gorgeous in a tuxedo, presented an award with his co-stars Shannen Doherty and Luke Perry. Then, only weeks later, Jason put his award-presenting shoes on again for the MTV Awards (which are for outstanding achievement in music video). Jason, again in a great-looking tuxedo, presented the award for "best alternative music video." The award went to one of J's fave bands, Jesus Jones ("Right Here, Right Now") and Jason was thrilled to be presenting to them. Afterwards, Jay revealed, "Jesus Jones is a cool bunch of guys; I dig their music and I'm really psyched that they won!"

Music happens to be another one of Jason's favorite things in the world! Jason is a big time fan of "The King Of Rock And Roll," Elvis Presley, and jokes, "I have an Elvis T-shirt that I've been trying to wear on "90210" for

Jason attended the premiere of *Young Guns II* with acress Robin Lively.

the longest time but they keep saying 'no' because it's too un-Brandon-like!"

Jason is also a mighty major fan of the other Elvis … Elvis Costello, that is! Elvis Costello is probably J's all-time favorite musician. J loves catching Costello in concert whenever he can and picks up every E.C. album as soon as it comes out! Some of Jason's favorite Elvis Costello tunes? He loves "Watching The Detectives," "Radio, Radio" and "Alison," but enjoys anything this rocking performer puts out! Elvis Costello's brand of music is referred to as alternative music. It's called that because it's an alternative to what is played on most top-40 stations. J's fave radio station is the alternative music station KROQ, in Los Angeles, which plays lots of exciting, new and foreign bands like Jesus Jones, EMF, Divynils and Seal.

When "90210" is on what's called a "hiatus," a week or more break in filming, Jason often heads for New York, where he has lots of friends. Jason can often be spotted hanging out at various hotspots on the Upper East Side. He meets his friends and they often dance the night away to alternative music! Jason also loves shopping in New York's Greenwich Village when he's in the Big Apple. Some fave stores include Canal Jean Co., Unique Boutique and Basic Basic, where he stocks up on wardrobe basics like jeans and tees and hunts for unusual antique jackets and vests. He also stops in at Tower Records to pick up the latest releases from all his fave bands.

No matter where Jason is, he has fave clubs. In Los Angeles his top shops include the Funky Fred Segal and various shops in off-beat Venice; and his fave places to munch out include the famous starspot, Hollywood Pizza Kitchen. Jason also loves driving up and down the coast of California with friends and going to places like Catalina Island, or even crossing the border into Mexico. His buds on "90210" are often along on J's drives, so if you're down in Tijuana, Mexico, and you see two dudes on motorcycles that look a whole lot like Jason

Jason takes a break during a charity ball game.

and Luke Perry ... you never know!

Other fave cities for Jason when he's got a bit of free time are London, England, and Las Vegas, Nevada. Jason's got an eye for fun in any town! In Vegas, he hangs out, checking the sights or taking in a show or boxing match. In fact, he and co-star, Ian Ziering made the trip to Nevada just for a prize fight! In England, in addition to visiting his sister, Jason hits the funky club scene and visits with friends he's made on previous trips. While in London, Jason spends much of his time

Just look into those heart-stopping, pulse-quickening eyes!

in public signing autographs. "90210" is the number-one show there! Jason and several other members of the cast made a recent trip there to pick up an award from Prince Edward!

As much as Jason likes to be a go-out-and-have-fun kind of guy, he also enjoys just hanging out with friends when he's in the mood. He loves reading and buys copies of everything from the classics to the latest best-sellers. Jason describes himself as being naturally curious and extremely interested in learning new things. Whether he's out on the town, renting a movie or reading the newest Stephen King book at home on a rainy day, one thing's for sure, Jason's the kind of guy who loves keeping busy when he's not working!

The last part of Jason's busy social schedule is perhaps the most important of all. No matter how busy he is, Jason always makes time for charity work. Currently, his pet charities include anything involving children. He continuously visits shelters and hangs out with the kids or spends time in hospitals with kids who have AIDS. Explains Jason, "I like to think that if I can reach one kid, I've done something!"

Besides visiting the kids, Jason also attends tons of celebrity fundraisers ranging from diabetes to the Starlight Foundation, an organization that grants wishes to critically ill children. Jason loves children and, like his counterpart, Brandon Walsh, feels that one of the most important things a person can do is get involved in solving the world's problems instead of just sitting in the back seat complaining about them.

JASON ON BRANDON

Becoming another person for sixty or seventy hours a week, forty or more weeks out of the year, is a very involved process! Jason Priestley does just that as he literally turns into Brandon Walsh for each and every episode of "Beverly Hills, 90210"! Just how much of a transformation is it for a dude from Canada to play a Minnesotan now living in Beverly Hills?

Jason has got at least one thing in common with Brandon Walsh, he too was once a transplanted teen! Really! You know that Brandon moved to the West Coast from the Midwest, but did you know that Jason also made quite a big move while still a teen? It's true. Upon graduation from high school, Jason packed his bags and moved all the way from his hometown of Vancouver, Canada, to California all by himself! And just what was it like for J to move to such a different place? He says, "Vancouver has more of a home-town feeling than Los Angeles does. The two cities are very different in size— Vancouver is much smaller. But I enjoy the weather and the people here in L.A. as much as I did in Vancouver."

So, like Brandon, Jason's move also consisted of going from a small town to a big city. And how about the culture shock the Walsh family encountered when they first set down stakes in sunny California; could Jason relate? Says Jason, "Definitely. Anytime you move from a place where you're living for a long time to another place that is very different, it takes a while to get adjusted." Hmmm ... just like Brandon!

Jason talks about how the culture shock he experienced from his move affected the way he's portrayed Brandon's experience with the very same thing. "I use some of what I went through in getting myself accustomed to L.A. to help me understand the way Brandon sees Beverly Hills after living in Minnesota," he says. We know how Brandon's move turned out, but what about Jason's? How has he adjusted to life in California? Is he a beach bunny? Laughs J, "I'm not really a beach person—I can't stand getting sand in my shoes. I miss the cold and snowy weather in Canada because I love winter sports."

We know that the Walshes almost packed it in and returned to Minnesota at the end of last season, but was there ever a point where Jason wanted to do that very same thing?

"I came to California knowing that I would stay until I reached my goal of working as an actor," says Jason. "Sometimes I really missed Vancouver, but I was doing exactly what I wanted to be doing." Though Jason admits he sometimes dislikes Los Angeles because, "It's a fast town, everything moves at an incredible pace," he concedes that its greatest feature is "it's easy to escape to somewhere quieter that has a slower pace to wind down and relax! Overall, I really enjoy living and working here—California is a great, fun place!" Bran-

Jason enjoys his California lifestyle.

don would agree!

Personality-wise, just ask anyone and they'll say Brandon and Jason are much more like distant cousins than the same person! J's co-star and good buddy Ian Ziering laughs, "I'd say when it comes to Jason and Brandon, he's pulling a stretch there!"

Carol Potter, who plays Jason's television mother, agrees. "Jason's much less of a 'good boy' than Brandon, and always was!" Jason explains, "When I was Brandon's age I wasn't really like him at all. I was much more 'the rebel without a clue' when I was in high school!"

We all know that Jason was a bit of a punker in school, sporting a mohawk, lots of black garb and motorcycle boots, and these days Jason still enjoys sporting a "rougher" look than his television counterpart. He's likely to grow his hair and a beard when he's not filming, and often sports a leather jacket or other un-Brandon like togs!

As for hobbies and pastimes, Jason and Brandon both enjoy reading and writing, as well as music, although we suspect that Jason's tastes are a bit more on the edge than Mr. Walsh's! Brandon's idea of a really great day is studying, going to class, hanging out and working, with maybe a date later in the evening! Jason's schedule generally includes either non-stop shooting days, or recreational days packed with thrill-seeking activities that Brandon would not take part in, like bungee jumping!

That's not to say that Brandon and Jason are entirely day and night. They do share some similar personality traits, like a great sense of humor, intelligence and a true romantic edge. So how does Jason feel about Brandon? Says J, "I like Brandon. I've got a soft spot in my heart for Brandon now. I'm having a good time with him."

So how much involvement does Jason really have in the kinds of things Brandon does week in and week out? Says Jason, "I have a lot of say. There isn't anyone who knows Brandon better than I do. I've been playing him for over a year now and I'm very at-home with him. Things will happen and I'll say, 'Brandon wouldn't do it that way. He'd probably do it this way.'" Continues J, "I also think Brandon's got a bit of a bad streak that just hasn't shown itself yet."

Hmmm ... But in the meantime, how does a rough-and-tumble dude like Jason play such a down-home dude as Brandon so perfectly? Ian Ziering sums it up, "Jason's just a really great actor!"

On-screen and off, Gabrielle Carteris and Jason are very good
friends.

A real-life daredevil, Jason catches some Z's in an unlikely place.

JASON: DROPPING HIM A LINE!

If, like many of Jason's fans, your feelings for him are much much too strong to keep to yourself, the time might be right to put pen to paper and let the J-man know exactly how you feel! Jason loves hearing from people who respect his work and are avid "90210" watchers! One thing is for sure, you're not the only J-fan with this plan ... at last count, Jason was receiving an average of 100 fan letters each and every day!

First, you've got to decide what you're trying to accomplish here. Are you trying to get an autographed picture or some kind of actual response? Most of you are probably screaming, "YES!" to the latter, right? If you're one of the zillions of folks trying to get Jason to write *you* back, then that's the first thing to keep in mind ... there *are* zillions of you! Taking that into consideration, you need to make your letter stand out.

You'll need to write neatly and clearly, using correct grammar and spelling. Jason can't reply if he can't even understand your writing! You'll also want to keep your letter or note short and to the point. Jason's really busy with his "90210" schedule and he's more likely to read something through if it's two paragraphs than if it's 200 pages! So keep stories about your biology teacher to a minimum ... save that stuff for another time!

Start your letter with something really interesting, or maybe a little offbeat. An example would be, "Did you know that tomatoes are really in the fruit family?" Okay, maybe that's a bit silly, but you get the idea. The idea is to make your letter different from the thousands that start out, "Hi Jason, how are you?" Another idea is to open your letter with a riddle or a joke ... don't forget Jason's got a great sense of humor. If you can start him out smiling, anything can happen!

If you are trying to request a picture, an autograph or something else specific, be clear about it! But be nice, too. "SEND ME A PICTURE NOW!" doesn't cut the mustard. Concluding your letter with a "P.S." asking for what you want is a good idea, it sets your question apart from the rest of your letter and makes the idea of wanting something seem like an afterthought. (For example, "As long as I'm writing could you drop me a B/W picture of yourself in the mail?")

If you are trying to get something back, enclose a self-addressed, stamped envelope if possible, maybe even a blank sheet of paper! Since Jason's so busy, why not have all the stuff he needs to answer your letter right there when he opens it? He won't have to go running for a stamp ... he can just jot something down and send it off!

Other ideas to get Jason to notice and read your letter once he's opened it include using funky homemade stationery and enclosing a brief poem, drawing or photo, even a stick of his fave gum (which, by the way, is bubble gum). (But never ever send an expensive gift through the mail ... who knows what may happen to it before it reaches its destination!) The main thing is to be creative and different. Your letter should look unique, and since you won't be there to see J in person, it should shout "you"!

It's also possible to write to Jason or any of your other fave stars without expecting something in return. If your feelings for Jason are just overflowing, or you're talking about him so much you're driving your best friend crazy, or you just adored the last episode of "90210", let your feelings flow onto some paper. Write as much or as little as you want, don't think about it, just let your pen or pencil rip! Sometimes the best writing is the kind that comes without a lot of thought. If you were Jason, wouldn't it just make your day to read a sweet letter from a real fan, who isn't asking for anything and just wanted to share her feelings? Sure! Or maybe after you've written a note, you won't even want to send it. Maybe you'll want to save it to look at later on or share with a friend. There's nothing wrong with writing a letter just to write one!

Once you've written a clear, original letter or note and are all set with anything you want to enclose ... then comes the key part, the packaging! There are lots of ways to make a letter or small package stand out and shout "OPEN ME!" at first glance, but first a list of "don'ts": Don't spray your mail with a ton of really strong perfume. Imagine what a crate of stinky mail smells like! Don't pucker up and seal your envelope with a kiss. Tons of gloppy, sticky lipstick-sealed envelopes stick together and make a really gross mess! And last,

Jason and Lou Diamond Phillips party hearty!

never, ever spell Jason's name incorrectly on the envelope!

Now, that you know what *not* to do, what should you do to get your mail noticed? Well, the most basic thing is color. Choose to send your Jason stuff in a standout color; it could be his fave color (black ... you can write on it with a paint marker), an unusual color or just a really cool and funky "notice me" color, like fuchsia! Next, the packaging you use can be a larger-sized envelope or an unusually shaped one, the type that makes the person looking at it say, "Hmmmm ... what could be in here???"

Next up, decoration with a capital "D". We're not talking about anything expensive, just something really creative. Why not keep in mind some of Jason's favorite things, like his motorcycle, sports or even his fave singer Elvis Costello? Come up with ideas for what to draw or stick on the envelope based on his faves and he's sure to recognize you as a true fan from the get-go! Also, and this is important, make sure if you are adhering anything onto your envelope or package, that you do so firmly. The last thing you want is stuff coming loose in the mail.

Okay, now you've got your mail written, packaged and ready to go, right? Well, not quite, you've got to address your letter first. You can get the most recent address for fan mail from the Fox network.

Have you written your return address clearly in the upper left hand corner? Good. Next, if your letter or package is heavier than a normal one, it's off to the local post office, where they'll weigh it for you and let you know the best way to send it. Why not pick out a cool stamp or two for it while you're there? Then, drop your Jason special in the mailbox and it's all over but the waiting (if you requested a reply).

One last bit of advice, as you go down to the mailbox every day looking for anything postmarked California. Nothing is guaranteed. Jason answers as much of his mail as he can, as do the people who assist him, but not every letter is answered. One thing is for sure, though; by following these easy steps you've put your best foot forward and done everything you can to make your fan mail successful. And who knows? One day you may be lazing around in your room watching MTV and your mother'll come in with the mail and yell, "There's something for you ... and its zip code is '90210'!"

JASON'S DREAMGIRL: DO YOU FIT THE BILL?

All Jason fans know that Mr. Priestley is currently unattached, but that doesn't mean he's not looking! Jason is very interested in finding that special gal to share good times. J's not the kind of guy who's so picky he has only one ideal gal in mind (Christie Brinkley, for example), but there are some basic qualifications for the lady who'll become the apple of Jason's eye! Curious to know just what J's dream girl is all about? Dying to

Nowadays, Jason is recognized wherever he goes—even in a market in England!

see if you fit the bill? Then read on!

First up, looks: Jason doesn't just go for girls who are model-like gorgeous. He's dated all kinds of ladies, blondes, brunettes, short, tall, long-haired, short-haired, freckled, un-freckled ... you name it! The most important thing to Jason, as far as appearances go, is overall attractiveness. He likes it when girls look put-together and neat. He appreciates it when a girl looks like she put some thought into her look for the day!

How a girl dresses and does her makeup and hair tells lots about her, too. Jason really loves it when a gal is versatile and can go from really casual (a pony tail and jeans) to completely dressy (an evening gown and hair in an upsweep). Mostly though, when it comes to how a person puts her look together, she should be comfortable with herself, and dressing to make herself happy. Jay hates it when girls dress just to impress him. He wants someone who feels the same way about her appearance as he does about his, natural! No gobs of makeup and big hair for girls who are gonna be with this guy, the J-ster's after a lady who can be herself!

One word here. Outdoorsy. As you know, Jason was born in Vancouver, Canada, and practically grew up in the great outdoors. His fave sport from childhood right on up to today is ice hockey—so if being bundled up to watch Jason play in the freezing cold sounds like a bore to you, think again! Jason also adores such outdoor sports as tennis, golf and rugby. Rain, snow or shine, you're likely to find Jason competing in or just watching outdoor sports! And speaking of those sports ... just how much do you know about them? Wouldn't it be great to converse with Jason about who won last night's NHL game? Study up! It's good to have a common subject to discuss with the guy of your dreams!

On the continuing subject of gals who love the great outdoors, Jason likes combining that with a love for doing things that are a bit off-beat and, in some cases, downright scary! Take for example his newfound hobby of bungee jumping. He and a pal (lately, Luke Perry) go to a bridge or high ground, strap a springy harness onto one ankle and ... gulp ... dive off! The cord is short enough to snap them back up before they hit the ground, but it supposedly feels like you're just hurtling through space! Even if it sounds a bit scary to you, Jason loves it. In fact, he videotapes his falls and watches them over and over again! If you're the type to get nervous about something like this maybe you should start bracing yourself!

Jason also is looking for a gal who loves whipping around in the open air on the back of his Yamaha motorcycle. Jason wears a helmet, of course, and you would have to as well. The thrill for him is being in pretty areas with nothing around him but nature! In fact, Jason typically loves taking roadtrips by bike to see new areas of the California coast. Hope you're not the kind of gal who'll be moaning about your hair being squashed by the helmet!

And be sociable! You don't have to be the biggest social butterfly in the world, but it's important to Jason that you're able to adapt to almost any social situation. Jason's life includes events as diverse as picnics with friends, televised award shows, and movie premieres! It's important to be able to smile and be friendly and comfortable around new people, as well as his old friends!

Diversity's the key to Jason's heart! Jason is an extremely complex guy. He's not the type who likes doing only one thing, or eating one thing, or hanging out at just one place. There are many different things he's interested in and lots of things he enjoys doing! Obviously, he would never expect you to love every one of his hobbies or friends, but he does consider himself an open-minded individual and would want you to be the same. For instance, he'd give a movie you wanted to see a shot, and would expect the same of you. Jason is not just about working hard on the set with his co-stars, or going out to premieres and charity events, or playing hockey, or watching a video, or reading or riding his

On the field or off, Jason always hits a homerun with fans.

bike, he's about all of them and much, much, more! All Jason would want from you is to have lots of things of your own going so he could try some of them, and you could try out some of the things he finds fun.

You'd better have a sense of humor. Jason's a really funny guy! Says his television mother Carol Potter, "Jason's always pulling pranks on the set," and Tori Spelling, his TV pal, "Jason is funny as anything, he cracks me up all the time!" Jason loves it when his friends laugh at his jokes, but he also loves it when someone comes up with really funny things on her own!

Be curious about some of Jason's favorite places in

the world. Other than his hometown of seven years, Los Angeles, Jason also loves New York. Remember, when there he goes shopping in the funky Soho/Greenwich Village area and checks out his fave bands at local clubs. Jason also adores Las Vegas—the people, the excitement and the craziness of it all, and he goes there whenever he can. Next on J's list of fave places to visit? Why, his birthplace ... Canada! Jason likes nothing better than dropping in on his family for a couple of days or hanging out with the old gang and playing a couple of quick games of hockey at the local pond! Last on Jason's globe o' travel fun? London, England! Jason's older sis lives there and "90210" is the top-rated program, but those aren't the only reasons he loves it. He likes the people and everything there is to see, but confesses "the food's not that great!" Since Jason loves to see the world so much, why not head on down to your local library and learn what you can about his fave spots?

Love music; Jason definitely does! Jason loves driving around in his truck with the radio blasting. So, bone up on his top 10, the two Elvis dudes, Presley and Costello, and alternative bands like Jesus Jones and The Replacements. Jason loves blasting his CD player but he's also into going to see his fave groups perform live and hang out with them backstage! How about heading on down to your local record store and listening to Elvis Costello's latest *Mighty Like A Rose.* Who knows? You just may love it!

Be informed! Jason is a very intelligent dude with a definite interest in the world around him. He watches the news daily and reads several newspapers to keep on top of current events. J often refers to topics like politics and the environment, and appreciates your ability to do the same! Jason also loves reading books about subjects which interest him and enjoys sharing whatever new ideas he's encountered. Check out a newspaper or book and learn about a new, interesting subject today.

Be interested in, but not obsessed with, his career. Jason obviously spends many hours on the set of "Beverly Hills, 90210" and has many interesting stories to tell about what goes on there. He likes his friends to

Surf's up for Luke and Jason, who are riding high on a tidal wave of success.

listen to what he has to say and really appreciates their advice and insight. On the other hand, Jason doesn't want a girl who'll do nothing but dwell on his job. Show business is just regular life for J and he doesn't want his friends reacting like everything he does is the greatest thing since sliced bread. Sure, being an actor is an interesting job, but to Jason what you do is really interesting, too.

Be sincere! Jason's main and final requirement for his dreamgirl is sincerity, someone who likes him for who he is! In the entertainment business, it can sometimes be a tricky thing to decide what people's intentions are. Performers often aren't sure if someone likes them for who they are or what their job is. Jason will want to know that you like *him,* so if just hanging out with a "star" is what you're after, forget about this guy!

JASON: BACK TO THE FUTURE!

The starring role in one of the most popular television shows on the air, being chosen as one of *People* magazine's "50 Most Beautiful People," appearing on the hottest talk shows, being a big-time teen idol, what does Jason think of it all? Well, to summarize Jason's feelings about his sudden "stardom," let's have a quote from the man himself: "I'm a working actor and that's about as far as it goes!"

Okay then, what does a working actor like J want to do in the future?

First off, expect Jason to stay on "Beverly Hills, 90210" as long as he can. Just ask any of the cast members, the whole "90210" gets along like one big, happy family. Basically, J's happy as a clam with the "Beverly Hills, 90210" bunch, and if the series continues enjoying the same success that it has recently, Jason would be perfectly happy to stick around as long as the producers want him!

Secondly, Jason does have some experience in feature films. He had roles in both "The Watchers" and "The Boy Who Could Fly" and enjoyed making both projects. Television is lots of fun for Jason, but he'd really enjoy the opportunity to portray and develop a different kind of character. Simply put, it's only a matter of time until Jason sets his sights on conquering the big screen the way he's conquered the small one!

Third, Jason is extremely interested in directing for television and is hoping to have the chance to direct an episode of "90210" as soon as he can! Jason feels he's completely qualified to direct for television; after all, he has been working in TV for the last 18 years or so! Being around lots of talented people behind the scenes has enabled J to pick up tons of valuable tips and skills for a future career in directing. How soon can we expect to hear Jason saying, "Action" and "Cut"? Chances are, it'll probably be awhile, since Jason's credo is "I want to master one craft (acting), before moving on to the next (directing)!"

In addition to directing, look for Jason to be penning a script or two in the future as well! The cast of "Beverly Hills, 90210" is quick to point out how open-minded the producers and writers of their show are to his ideas. Can it be long before Jason takes pen in hand and shares all his great ideas with the rest of us?

Relaxing at home.

Going back to college to take a few classes in subject matters that interest him is something that's likely for Jason as well. Jason is a voracious reader with interests in every field from religion to politics to science. Fact is, Jason loves learning about new things and discussing his thoughts and ideas with other people, but up until now he's been too busy with his career to register for classes and attend them!

What else does the future hold for Jason? Winning awards for his acting and maybe directing and writing ability? Probably. Taking classes or going back to school fulltime? Also a possibility. Spending lots of time kicking back and enjoying life? Definitely. Looking for and finding the girl of his dreams? Maybe. One thing is for sure, enjoying whatever it is he's doing and appreciating those who support him (that means you guys!) are high on Jason's list for next year and beyond!

JASON: HIS MAJOR MOMENTS

We all know where Jason Priestley is now: starring on a hugely popular television show. He's an idol to zillions of gals and just as many guys want to emulate him. But everyone knows you have to go from "Point A" to "Point B" to get to "Point C." In other words, there were some major markers in Jason's so-successful career!

★ At age 4, Jason begs his mom, a former dancer, to let him become an actor. She takes him to her former agent and he is signed immediately! Weeks later, Jay is working in national Canadian commercials!

★ At age 8, Jason lands his first major role! He is one of the key players in a Canadian television movie called "Stacey."

★ While growing up, Jason takes classes with Howard Fine and June Whitaker at the Neighborhood Playhouse.

★ After working continuously in Canada throughout his childhood, Jason decides to quit acting temporarily in high school and "just be a kid!" He shaves his head in a modified mohawk and spends his free time playing sports.

★ Upon graduation, Jason decides that acting is where his future lies and at the age of seventeen moves to Los Angeles. There, cushioned by the money he saved from working, he gets his first apartment.

★ In Los Angeles, Jason wins a continuous string of roles, beginning with bit parts in the television shows "Airwolf," "21 Jump Street," "Quantum Leap" and "MacGyver."

★ Jason supplements his television roles with stage work. He plays the role originated by Judd Nelson in "The Breakfast Club," as well as the James Dean role in "Rebel Without A Cause."

★ Jason nabs supporting roles in several feature films, including: "The Watchers" (co-starring Corey Haim), "The Boy Who Could Fly" and "Nowhere To Run."

★ 1988. Jason auditions for and wins the role of Todd Mahaffey in the pilot for a television show called "Sister Kate," about a nun who runs an orphanage.

★ "Sister Kate" gets picked up for the 1988-89 television season.

★ Despite some great reviews for Jason's performance and an already-growing audience of female fans (thanks to J!), "Sister Kate" is cancelled.

★ While Jason continues nabbing parts in television movies like "Lies From Lotus Land" and "Nobody's Child," "Sister Kate" is put into syndication and begins running episodes on several cable networks.

★ 1990. Aaron Spelling, the television genius behind programs such as "Vegas," "Charlie's Angels," "Fantasy Island" and "The Love Boat," comes up with the idea to do a television pilot about twins from Minnesota who must adapt to life in Beverly Hills.

★ With most of the performers cast, Spelling still has trouble looking for his lead, the male Walsh twin. He turns to his teenage daughter Tori for casting advice. Tori, an avid television watcher, recalls seeing "Sister Kate" and recommends that her father contact Jason.

Pictures, pictures and *no more* pictures, please!

★ Jason auditions for and wins the part of Brandon Walsh in the two-hour "Beverly Hills, 90210" pilot (then called "Class of Beverly Hills").

★ Late 1990, "90210" pilot movie airs.

★ Soon after, Fox TV picks up the show and orders an entire season of episodes.

★ Two of the other school-based shows on network television, "Hull High" and "Ferris Bueller" are dropped due to low ratings, while "90210" continues to build its share of the Thursday night audience despite the fact that it airs opposite the top-rated "Cheers."

★ College and high school students everywhere begin going crazy for the show. Jason and his co-star Luke Perry begin surfacing on the cover of teen magazines everywhere.

★ In an unprecedented move, Fox decides to air all-new episodes during the summer of 1991, when all other series are in reruns! The premiere summer episode of "90210" sweeps the ratings for the week it airs.

★ Jason begins receiving almost 100 fans letters daily.

★ Jason is named one of *People* magazine's "50 Most Beautiful People In The World!"

★ Jason appears on "Into The Night With Rick Dees" and "The Arsenio Hall Show."

★ Fall episodes begin airing as "90210" becomes a national obsession.

★ "90210" becomes the number-one show in the UK; Jason and several of the other cast members fly to England to accept an award from Prince Edward.

★ Jason appears as a presenter on both the MTV Awards Show and the Emmys.

★ Jason is chosen as one of *US* magazine's bachelors of the year.

Super-hunk incognito!

★ Jason makes appearances at fundraisers for Pediatric AIDS and various other children's charities.

★ Tomorrow and beyond ... who knows?

Super-hunks Jason and Luke—who's your #1?

JASON'S VERY VITAL STATS!

Full Name: Jason Priestley

Nickname: "J"

Height: 5'8"   **Weight:** 140 lbs.

Birthdate: 8/28/68

Birthplace: Vancouver, Canada

Current Residence: Woodland Hills, California

Family: Mom (Real Estate Agent), Dad (Textile Representative), Sister (18 months older, she lives in London)

Pets: A pot belly pig; Jason wants to get a hawk or falcon also

A FEW OF JASON'S FAVORITE THINGS

Transport: His Nissan Pathfinder and Yamaha motorcycle. Jason used to drive an Alfa Romeo sports car.

Colors: Black and Red

Footgear: Combat shoes

Cities: Los Angeles, New York, Las Vegas, and London, England

Food: Mexican and Chinese

Sports: Hockey, Basketball, Tennis, Bungee jumping, Rugby and Skiing

Hobbies: Reading, playing sports and listening to music

Radio Station: KROQ Los Angeles (alternative music)

Musicians: Elvis Presley, Elvis Costello and Jesus Jones (the group)

Actors: Robert Duvall, Al Pacino, Gary Oldman, Rutger Hauer, James Woods, John Savage and Dennis Hopper

JASON'S OH-SO QUOTABLE!

A few words of wisdom from the J-man.

On what he thinks is important about doing a show like "Beverly Hills, 90210":
"The episode we did on drunk driving struck a lot of chords with people. All of us have had friends and family members die as a result of drunk driving. I think the episode we did on AIDS hit home with a lot of people, too. We are not doing things that are outside the realm of possibility. We address these issues in a responsible manner that sets us apart!"

On the dumbest thing he ever read about himself:
"The dumbest thing I ever read about myself, I think was in a British paper. It was that I was a potato-picking-punk! The alliteration sounds good, but I had no idea what that meant!"

On what he thinks it takes to make it in show business:
"I think ambition and drive have a lot to do with it. If you stick it out and keep working—take the disappointment and the rejection and keep going, and keep your focus and drive, then you are going to rise above it."

On just what "Beverly Hills, 90210" is about:
"'Beverly Hills, 90210' is a show about growing up. A show about the kinds of problems teenagers face in the world today. It's a show about relationships and about family."

On Brandon Walsh:
"Brandon is half of a set of twins and he and his sister are very close. He's a good guy and has his feet planted firmly on the ground. He has a hold of his morals and values and a pretty good idea of what's going on. He's a good guy, a nice guy. He's a really nice guy!"

On why he thinks the "90210" writers have Brandon Walsh fall in love so much:
"I think it's pretty true to life. In high school you think

you fall in love every week, but you're not even really sure what love is."

On which he likes better, stage, television or movies:
"I think each one contains a lot of the things which I really enjoy. I don't think it's a question of which one I like better. I love them all! It's just that they're different."

On what he wants to do in the future:
"I want to keep going and keep improving and keep learning. I think that once you stop learning, you stagnate. You always have to try to improve yourself and go in new and exciting directions."

On watching himself on the screen:
"I have never been satisfied with any performance I have given. This forces me to improve, which is the most important thing, the reason I enjoy acting so much, that I can always improve."

On being considered one of the best-looking guys around:
"I never get up in the morning, look in the mirror and say 'Hey, J baby, looking good today.' I get up and say, 'Where's the Visine?'"

On the hardest part about doing "90210":
"I think the hardest part is driving in to work in the morning! But once I'm there it's fun, it's a definite pleasure!"

On his work with Pediatric AIDS and other children's charities:
"When I've got the time, I like trying to help out if I can. I feel like if I can just get one kid to smile, then I've really accomplished something."

On his image in high school:
"I had kind of a mohawk. I jumped on the tail end of the punk movement. I had chains, black jeans and combat boots!"

On the hype now surrounding the show:
"I try not to listen to things like that. I don't like anything detracting from my focus and what I'm doing."

On being a teen star:
"A what?"

On playing super good guys:
"I like playing good guys. Actually, I only started playing good guys in the last couple of years. Up until then I used to play bad guys. I used to play really hard, bad guys."

On Brandon Walsh's hidden bad streak:
"I think Brandon's got a bad side ... everyone does. We saw a little flash of it in the episode where he screwed up by getting drunk and crashing his car ... I think there's more."

On how his family and friends are reacting to his success:
"My family is really excited and happy. And my friends ... well, most of my friends are actors and they are completely psyched for me, too!"

ALL ABOUT JASON

Jason Priestley's "Beverly Hills, 90210" co-stars have lots to say about him.

Gabrielle Carteris, who plays Brandon's bud/sometime crush, Andrea Zuckerman::
"He's the greatest. We have an exceptional cast. Jason's obviously cute, but he's also very supportive, loving and a great actor. It's wonderful working with him!"

Brian Austin Green, who plays the school's former nerd-in-residence, David Silver:
"I'm a drummer. I love playing the drums and Jason plays, also. Mostly we do a lot of talking about playing the drums and music that we like. He's a lot of fun, and a good guy!"

Jason and TV sibling Shannen Doherty amid the madness of the
Primetime Emmy Awards.

Ian Ziering, who plays Steve Sanders, Brandon's other bud:

"We all acknowledge that J's the man. He's basically the show's quarterback and thank God for him because he's doing a great job! There are absolutely no hostilities about that at all. I'm glad he's in the driver's seat. Also, the fact that Jason isn't a whole lot like Brandon in real life and plays him so well is a real testament to his acting. He's good! Plus, he's a fun guy in real life. We hang out, in fact we just went to a boxing match last week. He's a real good guy!"

Tori Spelling, who plays Donna Martin:

"He's like my older brother. He's cute, but I never notice. Yet when I bring my friends onto the set that's who they always want to meet—Jason!"

Shannen Doherty, who plays Brandon's twin, Brenda:

"Jason is gorgeous ... he has those eyes, but he's very guarded, he doesn't like for people to see his vulnerability. With a show like ours, you can't help but get on each other's nerves sometimes, but that's good, too, because it's kind of like a brother and sister deal. Jason and I work so closely together that we'll get annoyed at each other and then it'll be okay. Just like real brothers and sisters do!"

Carol Potter, who plays Brandon's mom, Cindy:

"I look at him and I'm very impressed. I respect him! I think Jason's like Brandon in a lot of ways, maybe not in his behavior, though ... Jason's a bit crazier than Brandon and always was!"

100 KEY JASON PRIESTLEY FACTS!

1. Jason's birthsign is Virgo.

2. Jason's first major job was a Canadian television movie called "Stacey."

3. Jason has a sister, eighteen months older than he, who studies dance in London.

4. Jason's favorite foods are Chinese and Mexican.

5. Jason's career started with commercials at age 4.

6. Jason has a pot belly pig as a pet.

7. Jason plays on a semi-pro hockey team against NHL veterans.

8. Singer Elvis Costello is Jason's all-time fave performer.

9. Jason starred as orphan Todd Mahaffey on "Sister Kate."

10. Jason plays the drums.

11. Jason's fave footwear is combat boots.

12. When he's on hiatus from "90210," Jason likes to grow his hair and a beard.

13. Jason loves Las Vegas.

14. Jason quit acting when he was in high school.

15. Jason goes bungee jumping with co-star Luke Perry.

16. Jason's friends call him J.

17. Jason drives a Nissan Pathfinder.

18. Jason wants to get a hawk or falcon for a pet.

19. Jason's mom is a real estate agent in Vancouver.

20. Jason presented an award to British band Jesus Jones on MTV's awards show.

21. Jason has been living in California since 1987.

22. Jason loves golfing and playing tennis.

23. Jason's fave color is black.

24. Jason's roommate is an actor named David Merill.

25. Jason can be seen tooling around on his Yamaha motorcycle.

26. Jason's dad is a manufacturer's representative for a furniture and textile company.

27. Before his Pathfinder, Jason drove a sporty Alfa Romeo.

28. Jason is a really big fan of Elvis Presley.

29. When visiting New York, Jason hangs out on the Upper East Side.

30. Jason's fave actors include Robert Duvall, Al Pacino, Gary Oldman, Dennis Hopper, John Savage, Rutger Hauer and James Woods.

31. Jason loves going to the movies.

32. Jason and co-star Ian Ziering often go to prize fights.

33. Jason was born on August 28, 1968.

34. Jason had a major role in the Disney Channel's serials "Teen Angel" and "Teen Angel Returns."

35. Jason lives in a three-bedroom house.

36. Jason's grandfather was a circus acrobat.

37. Jason was born in Vancouver, Canada.

38. Jason's fave radio station is KROQ.

39. Jason's got two step-sisters.

40. Jason's mom was a ballerina.

41. Jason loves playing basketball and rugby.

42. Jason makes his home in a town in California called Woodland Hills.

43. Jason volunteers for many children's charities.

44. Jason loves the great outdoors.

45. Jason used to have a dog but it ran away.

46. Jason loves going to movie premieres.

47. When in New York, Jason hangs out at Ruby's.

48. According to his co-stars, Jason's got a great sense of humor.

49. Jason loves to cook, his specialty is fajitas.

50. Tori Spelling recommended Jason for the part of Brandon.

51. Jason had a bit part on "21 Jump Street."

52. Jason loves wearing funky antique jackets.

53. Jason presented an award at The Emmys with Luke Perry and Shannen Doherty.

54. Co-star Ian Ziering refers to Jason as the "quarterback" of "90210."

55. J reveals that the one thing that's always in his fridge is ketchup.

56. In Los Angeles, Jason hangs out with co-star Luke Perry.

57. Jason appeared on "The Arsenio Hall Show."

58. Jason had a bit part on the TV show "Quantum Leap."

59. Jason loves snow skiing.

60. Jason was chosen as one of *People* magazine's "50 Most Beautiful People."

61. Jason jokes that the hardest part of his job is "driv-

ing to work."

62. Shannen Doherty, who plays J's sis, Brenda, reveals that the two sometimes argue in real life like a brother and sister.

63. Jason had a bit part on the television show "Airwolf."

64. Jason played the Judd Nelson role in a stage version of "The Breakfast Club."

65. Jason is close pals with Robin Lively of "Doogie Howser, MD."

66. Jason refers to his co-star Luke Perry as his "partner in crime"!

67. When he's got time, Jason attends fundraisers for all sorts of children's charities.

68. Jason says his mother instilled in him "a great sense of independence."

69. Jason's very sarcastic!

70. Jason's three fave things about acting are: "the excitement, the people and the fact that you can never be perfect at it—you can always improve."

71. Jason adores water sports like sailing.

72. Jason loves practical jokes!

73. Jason believes in being loyal to his friends and feels that if you are mean to someone behind their back, it's "bad karma."

74. Carol Potter, who plays Jason's television mom, says he's "the biggest wisecracker on the set!"

75. Jason confesses he was "nothing like Brandon as a teen" and insists he was more of a "rebel without a clue"!

76. Jason has lots to say about what Brandon does and

Jason, Shannen and Luke were presenters at the 43rd Annual Emmy Awards show, held at the Pasadena Civic Center in 1991.

doesn't do on "90210" and the writers usually listen to his opinion.

77. Jason had featured roles in the made-for-television films, "Lies From Lotus Land" and "Nobody's Child."

78. Jason got his acting training at the Neighborhood Playhouse.

79. Jason loves beat-up Levi's and T-shirts.

80. Jason loves sleeping in on weekends.

81. Jason appeared in the feature film "The Watchers" with Corey Haim.

82. Jason had his hair cut in a modified mohawk style when he was in high school.

83. Jason is close to his sister and visits her in London whenever he can.

84. Jason appeared in the stage version of "Rebel Without A Cause."

85. Jason believes that, "In high school you fall in love once a week but you're not even sure what love's all about."

86. Jason says he likes playing good guys but before playing Todd on "Sister Kate," he only used to play bad guys.

87. Jason loves getting dressed up in a tux for special occasions.

88. Jason has been a guest on "Into The Night."

89. Jason was able to make a living at acting as soon as he moved out to California.

90. Jason loves cruising the California highways on his motorcycle, and sometimes plans overnight trips with co-star and fellow cycler Luke Perry.

91. Stephanie Beacham, who was J's co-star on "Sister Kate," now plays Dylan's mom on "90210."

92. Jason says that when he was growing up, every show he watched was produced by Aaron Spelling, who now produces "Beverly Hills, 90210."

93. On weekends, Jason says he "just hangs out"!

94. Jason gets an average of 100 fans letters daily.

95. Jason appeared in the flick "The Boy Who Could Fly."

96. Jason's acting teachers were Howard Fine and June Whitaker.

97. Jason appeared in the feature film "Nowhere To Run."

98. Jason's been acting professionally for twenty years!

99. Jason was named MVP on every hockey team he played on.

100. Jason loves winter sports.

JASON'S TRICKY TRIVIA

★

JUST JASON

1. The name of the character which Jason played on the television show "Sister Kate" was: **a)** Jeff Bridges **b)** Todd Mahaffey **c)** Brandon Walsh **d)** none of the above

2. How old was Jason when he signed with his first agent and began his career? **a)** three **b)** twenty-three **c)** five **d)** none of the above

3. What sport does Jason play in a local league? **a)** rugby **b)** golf **c) hockey d)** bocce ball

4. Jason starred in which of these movies on the Disney Channel? **a)** "Teen Angel" **b)** "Teen Angel Returns" **c)** both a and b **d)** none of the above

5. Which of these television awards shows was Jason a presenter on? **a)** *The Emmy Awards* **b)** *The Tony Awards* **c)** *The Academy Awards* **d)** none of the above

6. Jason was born in which Canadian city? **a)** Montreal **b)** Quebec **c)** Vancouver **d)** Los Angeles

7. What kind of car does Jason currently drive? **a)** BMW **b)** Isuzu Trooper **c)** Nissan Pathfinder **d)** Alfa Romeo

8. Which of his "90210" co-stars does Jason go bungee jumping with? **a)** Carol Potter **b)** Tori Spelling **c)** Luke Perry **d)** Ian Ziering

9. In which European city does Jason's older sister live? **a)** Paris **b)** Munich **c)** Stockholm **d)** London

10. What musical instrument does Jason play? **a)** drums **b)** guitar **c)** the recorder **d)** the triangle

★

"90210" TO GO

Match each of the "90210" actors/actresses on the left with the part they play!

1. Brian Austin Green   **A.** Steve Sanders
2. Doug Emerson   **B.** Kelly Taylor
3. James Eckhouse   **C.** Scott Scott
4. Carol Potter   **D.** Brandon Walsh
5. Shannen Doherty   **E.** Donna Martin
6. Ian Ziering   **F.** David Silver
7. Jason Priestley   **G.** Dylan McKay
8. Jennie Garth   **H.** Brenda Walsh
9. Tori Spelling   **I.** Jim Walsh
10. Luke Perry   **J.** Andrea Zuckerman
11. Gabrielle Carteris   **K.** Cindy Walsh

Which "90210" character did each of these incidents happen to on the show?

1. This character lives outside the school district and secretly takes a bus every morning.

2. This character subbed for Brandon as a waitress at The Peach Pit.

3. This character was in a surfing accident.

4. This character left for the summer to visit his grandparents in Oklahoma.

5. This character did poorly on the SATs because of a learning disability called dyslexia.

6. This character was Brandon's co-manager for a Little League baseball team.

7. This character's mother is dating David Silver's dad.

8. This character is the school's deejay.

9. This character went to the Spring dance with Kelly.

10. This character found out last season that he is adopted.

★
ANSWERS

Just Jason: 1.) b 2. d 3. c 4. c 5. a 6. c 7. c 8. c 9. d 10. a

Character matching: 1.) F 2.) C 3.) I 4.) K 5.) H 6.) A 7.) D 8.) B 9.) E 10.) G 11.) J

Which character:
1.) Andrea Zuckerman
2.) Brenda Walsh
3.) Dylan McKay
4.) Scott Scott
5.) Donna Martin
6.) Steve Sanders
7.) Kelly Taylor
8.) David Silver
9.) Brandon Walsh
10.) Steve Sanders